SPECIALS!

The Twentieth-Century World
British Democracy

Mary Green

Acknowledgements

The author and publisher would like to thank the following for permission to reproduce photographs and other material:

Greater London Photograph Library	45D
Hulton Deutsch Collection	12B, 15D, 20B, 23A
Illustrated London News Picture Library	15C, 37, 39B
Manchester City Art Galleries/ Bridgeman Art Library, London	20A
Mansell Collection	14A, 18A, 40C, 46C
Museum of London	front cover, 8C, 9A
National Museum of Ireland	36C
National Museum of Labour History	41C
Picturepoint, London	16, 36A
Popperfoto	38A, 39C
Punch	7B, 12C, 22, 23B, 24C, 31, 42A, 42B, 44B, 44C
Solo Syndication/CSCC	25A, 33B
The Rank Organisation plc	21C
The Spectator/CSCC	26
Topham Picture Source	9B, 39A

The front cover shows Mrs Pankhurst being arrested during a suffragette demonstration on 21 May 1914.

The publisher has made every effort to contact copyright holders. If any have been overlooked, we will be pleased to make any necessary arrangements.

Folens books are protected by international copyright laws. All rights reserved. The copyright of all materials in this book, except where otherwise stated, remains the property of the publisher and author(s). No part of this publication may be reproduced, stored in a retrieval system, or transmitted, in any form or by any means, for whatever purpose, without the written permission of Folens Limited.

Folens do allow photocopying of selected pages of this publication for educational use, providing that this use is within the confines of the purchasing institution.

This resource may be used in a variety of ways; however, it is not intended that teachers or students should write directly into the book itself.

Mary Green hereby asserts her moral right to be identified as the author of this work in accordance with the Copyright, Designs and Patents Act 1988.

© 1994 Folens Limited, on behalf of the author.

First published 1994 by Folens Limited, Albert House, Apex Business Centre, Boscombe Road, Dunstable, LU5 4RL, England.

ISBN 1 85276605-0

Editor: Ian Jenkins
Illustrations: Tonia Thorne

Printed by Ashford Colour Press

Contents

Teachers' Notes

Title	Purpose
The Franchise	
Wife and Servant	An introduction to the franchise. Pupils could note the differences and similarities between the lives of middle- and working-class women. When discussing fact and opinion, the pupils could also examine the background information at the top of the sheet.
Women's Rights	The focus is on the slow pace of change in the position of women. The usefulness of source C as a means of illustrating women's inequality could be further discussed.
Deeds Before Words	These activities continue from the previous sheet. Pupils could comment on the usefulness of source B in locating information on the NUWSS. Some pupils could investigate further the different tactics employed by the WSPU and the NUWSS and then make a databank of their findings.
Votes For Women 1 and 2	Use both sheets together. The focus on these pages is on historical interpretation and the selection of historical sources, since all the sources are memoirs and were published well after the events to which they refer. However, some pupils could discuss the advantages and disadcantages of the use of certain kinds of written material as secondary historical sources.
Different Views 1 and 2	Use both sheets together. Pupils could focus on the different ideas and attitudes and the usefulness of different sources. They could also compare their own interpretations of sources. Some pupils could discuss the reliability and usefulness of source C in relation to the circumstances in which it was produced.
New Tactics 1 and 2	Use both sheets together. Pupils are encouraged to recognise that cause and consequence vary in importance and to identify a range of attitudes. Usefulness and reliability of sources are also important points for discussion. Extension work could involve searching for similar sources.
Cat and Mouse	This sheet is simpler than the previous two, but could be taught in conjunction with them. Pupils are asked to extract and infer information and to distinguish between fact and opinion. Work on the database will need to be done in pairs.
Women and War	Pupils are asked to recognise that change can be rapid or slow and most importantly that progress and change are not necessarily synonymous. Some pupils could be encouraged to assess the effects of the First World War on the franchise. They could begin by listing reasons for the extension of the franchise under two headings: 'important' and 'not very important'.
Changes in the Political Party System	
Greater Democracy	Some pupils may need help with judging the reliability of source A and assessing its value in highlighting the issue of poverty (photographs such as this could have been posed, but even so their value as historical sources should not be overlooked). Relating the Reform Acts to better social conditions is difficult but simple deductions from the information could be made.
The Commons Versus the Lords	Pupils will need to be aware of the power held by the Lords at this time, the different political attitudes involved and the consequences of the Liberals gaining power. Pupils could investigate further the power vested in the monarchy at the time.
Poverty and Hardship 1 and 2	Use both sheets together. The romanticised view of the working class and the notion of the 'dignity of work' could be addressed when pupils have recognised basic differences between sources A and B. Source C is interesting as a secondary source and Mayhew's comment in source D gives ideas for extension work. All these sources lend themselves to more sophisticated enquiry.
The Rise of Socialism	A basic understanding of socialism can allow inference to be made about the cartoon. The view of the cartoonist and the significance of the source could be discussed. Pupils could construct their own cartoon or collage to communicate what they know. Another discussion point could be the reasons why immigrant communities of this period have been largely ignored by historians.
Divide and Fall	The contrast between sources A and B demonstrates how the selection of sources can give a different historical perspective.
Right, Left and In-Between	Connections could be made between source C (the idea of 'mixing' to make a coalition) and the two-party system, with one party in power and the other in opposition. Pupils could be asked to consider more closely why coalitions tend to fail.
The 1945 Election	The extent to which these sources simplify the cause of Labour's victory needs to be discussed. Pupils could investigate the other reasons for the victory.
Post-War Change	The emphasis on this sheet is on rapid social change, although pupils may have difficulty in recognising this. Macmillan's slogan 'you've never had it so good' could be introduced, and pupils could investigate whether this was true for all people. Sources which deal with post-war social problems (e.g. homelessness and poverty in Ken Loach's *Cathy Come Home*, 1966) could be used to broaden the discussion. The activity sheets on the Welfare State could be used.

© Folens.

Title	Purpose
Democratic and Non-Democratic Systems	
What is Democracy?	This sheet encourages understanding by asking pupils to investigate voting habits amongst young people.
Constitutions and Rights	Extension work could involve a simple questionnaire involving people's views of the Theresa Bennett case and its implications.
Proportional Representation	This sheet could be used in conjunction with 'Catholics and Protestants'.
The Presidential System	Extension work could involve discussion of the way in which cartoons give a limited historical view, but may also highlight the central issue. This cartoon reverses the normal assumption that people will try to prevent a suicide, leading to questions about democratic power and responsibility.
The One-Party System	Comparisons between the one- and two-party system could expand discussions on the nature of democracy. The glossary should be made available.
How Democratic is Democracy?	Some pupils may need some help with references in the cartoon and its caption. Extension work could examine the implication that the media is biased against the left. Pupils could also note that cartoons are themselves part of the media.
Northern Ireland, Eire and the UK	
Conflict in Ireland	This and the following activity sheet could be taught in conjunction. Pupils will need to connect the 'grim warning' in source C with the information in sources A and B. A basic recognition of the polarised political situation in Ireland is important.
Catholics and Protestants	Some pupils might be able to connect source C on the previous sheet and source A on this sheet. Source B could be examined for bias. Its usefulness in illustrating a popular view could also be discussed. Source C could be used to examine the nature and purpose of secondary sources.
Home Rule and the Easter Rising	Some pupils will be able to identify a long-term consequence of the Easter Rising. Other pupils could identify short-term consequences. Reference to the text and a general understanding of the events leading to the Easter Rising are important.
Partition	The glossary will need to be used. A clear (if basic) understanding of partition is necessary. The map of 'Conflict in Ireland' could be referred to. The usefulness of the photograph as an illustration of commitment to a cause could be discussed. Pupils could discuss the possible reasons for the photographer's choice of picture as part of a discussion of how circumstances affect the reliability and value of a source.
Civil Rights/ Ireland's Future	These need to be taught in conjunction. When discussing the voting system it may be useful to refer to 'How Democratic is Democracy?' and 'Proportional Representation'. Selecting one source to make two posters with opposite meanings can help pupils demonstrate how historical interpretations depend on the selection of sources.
The People and the State	
The Growth of Trade Unions	Some background knowledge of the period will be needed. 'The Rise of Socialism' could be referred to. Inference as well as simple deductions need to be made, particularly when using source C (the similarity of the figure to a French revolutionary (sansculotte) will need to be pointed out). Pupils could consider how such information affects their judgement of the source.
The General Strike	Questions of the usefulness and reliability of historical sources are introduced on this sheet, particularly with regard to source B. Pupils could investigate the author's selection of sources and discuss out what they do not show. Further discussion could revolve around the long- and short-term political and social consequences of the volunteers' actions.
Unions and the State: the 1970s	When pupils have understood the sources at a basic level they could attempt to evaluate their usefulness. Discussion could include what the sources indicate about the period and about the relationship between unions and government. Pupils' attention should be drawn to the impact of Edward Heath's Industrial Relations Act 1971, which limited union power.
The Beveridge Report	This is best taught in conjunction with the next two activity sheets. Comparisons could be made between the intentions behind the setting up of the Welfare State in the 1940s and the range of consequences, both long term and short term.
The National Health Service	The previous sheet assumes complete support for the Welfare State. On this sheet the sources show a variety of attitudes, and raise questions about the similarity of past and more recent attitudes.
A Decent Standard of Living?	Exercises using source D and the 'Find Out' activity could be used to show how interpretations of the past can depend on sources. This could be broadened into a discussion about the use of historical sources for different purposes (see Introduction). Extension work could involve further interviews, and a range of interpretations could be examined.
Public and Private	This activity sheet is largely self-explanatory. Pupils will need to have acquired some knowledge about nationalisation in order to make comments on the usefulness of source C. Extension work could involve making a cartoon or poster presenting the opposite view.

Introduction

How to use this book
The activity sheets in this book are designed to provide additional support for pupils experiencing learning difficulties at key stage three and above. The book deals with the focal events and issues in British democracy from 1900 to approximately 1975.

The sheets are designed to introduce complex concepts in an accessible format. The topics will require background explanation, since the pupils will need an awareness of the context of each topic before the activities can be attempted. The sheets are designed to supplement existing courses, and are not intended as a course in themselves.

Throughout the book there is particular emphasis on examining historical sources. There is a dual benefit in this approach:

- it encourages valid historical tasks; sources can be used to extrapolate information, to exemplify the text, and most importantly to focus both on the variety of ways in which history has been presented and on the value of the sources themselves
- it depends less heavily on the use of text, since pupils with learning difficulties often find text discouraging even when it is within their capabilities.

The topics do not have to be taught in sequence. Pupils should be encouraged to approach the more difficult concepts – for instance, recognising that historical sources are problematic and should be viewed critically. Literacy difficulties do not necessarily mean limited understanding and where possible pupils should look at issues in depth as well as in outline. The activities should be used in such a way as to avoid stereotypical answers and to encourage more sophisticated enquiry, e.g. the reliability of sources and the validity of artistic impressions.

Many of the sheets encourage development of the activities by the pupils themselves. In particular, pupils should be encouraged to undertake further research on specific issues discussed on the sheets and draw upon their knowledge in order to produce extended pieces of writing.

Sources
The sources used throughout the book are varied, including cartoons, photographs and quotations, from both the period under discussion and later historical accounts. It is important that pupils recognise the difference between primary and secondary sources and understand that the study of history involves the use of both types of source. The activities on the sheets encourage the evaluation of both primary and secondary sources, while the extension activities involve further investigation of secondary sources, such as extracting information and evaluating its validity. Pupils should be encouraged to combine the use of both types of source and to recognise that this method of studying history allows them to reach valid and reasoned conclusions.

Pupils should also be encouraged to develop an awareness of the use of different types of source, e.g. newspaper reports, autobiographical accounts and artists' impressions, and their implications. Another issue that pupils are invited to consider is the reliability and value of the sources, which could be broadened into a discussion of the use of historical sources for different purposes. Pupils should be encouraged to recognise the difference between historiography (the use of sources in historical accounts), and propaganda (the manipulation of sources for specific political purposes).

The glossary
Key words are highlighted in bold on each sheet and are listed in a separate box. These words can be found in the glossary. This should be copied and made available to pupils for regular use, since many of the concepts and terms used in the book are complex.

Paired and oral work
Many of the activities could involve pupils working in pairs with a high degree of oral work. The significance of paired and oral work cannot be over-emphasised. Discussion of the issues raised in the book encourages the exchange of ideas and promotes further investigation.

 © Folens.

Wife and Servant

Background

At the start of the nineteenth century women were not seen as individual citizens, but the property of their husbands. Women in poor families worked long hours in factories, down pits or on the land, even when pregnant. They took in washing and sewing. Their children often worked with them. Most **middle-class** women did not work. Husbands were expected to keep their wives, and wives were expected to look after the house. Daughters received some education but usually to prepare them for marriage. Rich or poor, women were dependent on men.

Key Words

middle class
working class

A

Wife and Servant
are the same,
But only differ
in the name.

(From *To the Ladies* by Lady Chudleigh, 1703.)

B

Rich and poor: a cartoon from Punch, *1861.*

Activities

Look at source A.

1. What do you think Lady Chudleigh meant when she said this?
2. Are her words fact or opinion?
3. How could you find out if other people agreed with her?
4. Do you think she came from a rich or a poor family? Give a reason for your answer.

Look at source B.

5. Describe what each picture shows.
6. Which woman is poor and which better off?
7. Explain what you think *Punch* meant by 'pin money' and 'needle money'.
8. Use the information on this page to list five points about the lives of **working-class** and middle-class women. Draw a chart like this:

	working-class women	middle-class women	supporting information
1.			
2.			
3.			
4.			
5.			

9. Write whether source **A** or **B** or the background supports each point.

Women's Rights

Background

During the nineteenth century women began to gain greater independence. **Acts of Parliament** brought about changes or **reforms**.

Key Words

Act of Parliament
middle class
reform
working class

A

The Position of Women in 1800

- Women could not:
  - vote
  - own property
  - sign contracts.
- Women had no rights:
  - over their children
  - over their own bodies
  - over their earnings.

B

Some Reforms

1870
A wife could keep her own earnings.

1873
Cambridge University took women students.

1876
Medical colleges took women students.

1880
Married women could own property.

1886
On her husband's death a woman became the legal parent.

1891
Women could no longer be kept prisoners at home by their husbands.

1894
A woman could be a parish or district councillor.

C

What a Woman may be, and yet not have the Vote
MAYOR NURSE MOTHER DOCTOR or TEACHER FACTORY HAND
What a Man may have been, & yet not lose the Vote
CONVICT LUNATIC Proprietor of white Slaves Unfit for Service DRUNKARD

Poster in support of women's rights, 1910.

Activities

Compare the information in A and B.

1. What changed between 1800 and 1894?
2. What did not change?
3. Which reforms would be most important to:
   - a **middle-class** married mother
   - her unmarried daughter?
4. What changed for **working-class** women?

Look at source C.

5. What point is the poster making?
6. Who would have made a poster like this?
7. Why was this poster made?
8. What did the designers of the poster want people to think?

 © Folens.

Deeds Before Words

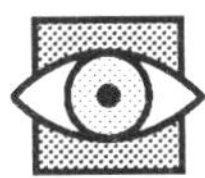

Background

By the end of the nineteenth century more and more men had been given the right to vote in **elections**. Women had been asking for the vote for many years. The **NUWSS (National Union of Women's Suffrage Societies)** was formed in 1897 to campaign for the vote for women. NUWSS members were called suffragists. They had little success, so in 1903 Emmeline Pankhurst formed the more **militant WSPU (Women's Social and Political Union)**. Members of this group were called **suffragettes**.

Key Words

election **NUWSS** **WSPU**
militant **suffragette**

Activities

Look at source A

1. What does it tell you about the aims of the WSPU?
2. Would it have been an effective logo in 1903? Give reasons for your answer.
3. Find out more about the aims of the WSPU, then design your own WSPU logo to show these aims.
4. The WSPU did not campaign only for the vote. List three other rights for women that might have concerned them.
5. Have these concerns changed over the years or not?
6. List three rights which concern women today. Compare your answers with a partner.

Look carefully at source B.

7. The NUWSS was not as militant as the WSPU. Explain what this means.
8. How important was this difference? Give reasons for your answer.

Find Out

Find out as much as you can about the two groups and write about the main differences.

A

WSPU logo, 1903.
Their motto was 'Deeds Before Words'.

B

NUWSS march to London, 1913.

Votes for Women 1

Background

During the **election** campaign in 1905, Sir Edward Grey of the **Liberal Party** made a speech at the Free Trade Hall in Manchester. Christabel Pankhurst (Emmeline Pankhurst's daughter) and Annie Kenney, members of the **Women's Social and Political Union (WSPU)**, were there.

Key Words

election
Liberal Party
suffragette
WSPU

A

Annie Kenney stood up in her chair and cried out: "Will the Liberal Government give votes to women?" The audience became a mob. They howled, they shouted and roared ... Hands were lifted to drag her out of her chair but Christabel helped ward off the mob, who struck and scratched at her until her sleeve was red with blood.

(From *My Own Story* by Emmeline Pankhurst, 1914.)

B

Christabel thrust Annie forward to ask: "Will the Liberal Government give women the vote?" ... Annie Kenney was dragged down by the men sitting near her and one of the stewards put a hat over her face. Christabel repeated the question. The hall was filled with conflicting cries: "Be quiet!" ... "Let the lady speak!" ... Annie stood on her chair to ask again, whilst Christabel strove to prevent her removal.

(From *The Suffragette Movement* by Sylvia Pankhurst, 1931.)

Activities

Read carefully sources A and B.

1. Find three differences between the sources. Draw a chart like this and write them in.

	A	B
1. 2. 3.		

Look carefully at the dates of sources A and B.

2. How many years after the event was each book written?

3. Does this mean that one source is more reliable than the other because of when it was written?

 © Folens.

Votes for Women 2

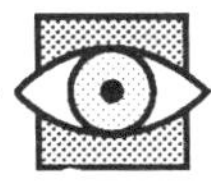

Background

Christabel Pankhurst and Annie Kenney were arrested during the meeting. They refused to pay their fines and went to prison. The newspapers reported the incident the next day.

C

On the night of the meeting Christabel set out with Annie Kenney to heckle the coming Liberal minister. "I shall sleep in prison tonight!" she gaily said.

(From *The Suffragette Movement* by Sylvia Pankhurst, 1931.)

D

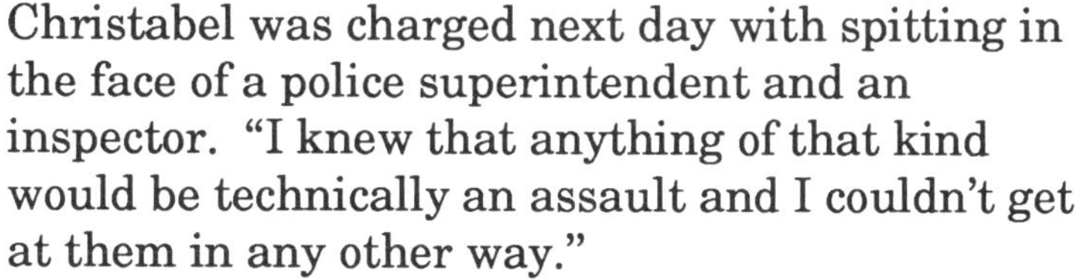

Christabel was charged next day with spitting in the face of a police superintendent and an inspector. "I knew that anything of that kind would be technically an assault and I couldn't get at them in any other way."

(From *The Suffragette Movement* by Sylvia Pankhurst, 1931.)

Activities

Read carefully the extracts from Sylvia Pankhurst's book (sources B (page 10), C and D).

1. Draw a chart like this and complete it. Use all three sources.

Event			
Place			
Members of WSPU there	Action	Outcome	Source

Read sources C and D.

2. Why do you think Christabel wanted to be arrested?

3. Do you think the actions of the WSPU speeded up or prevented women getting the vote? Give reasons for your answer.

Different Views 1

Background

Not all women were in favour of the vote. Not all men were against it.

A

Queen Victoria was a strong opponent of women's rights, which she looked upon as a kind of 'mad, wicked folly'.

(From *Strong-Minded Women* by Janet Murray, 1982.)

B

A procession to Hyde Park, 1908.

Activities

Read source A.

1. How might Queen Victoria's views have influenced support for women's rights?

Look at source B.

2. The banner says 'Women's Will Beats Asquith's Won't'. What does this mean?
3. Who was Asquith?
4. Did he support women's rights? Give reasons.
5. Would men who did not support women's rights have joined in this procession? Why?

Look at source C.

6. Some people said that the women who fought for equal rights really wanted to be like men. How does source **C** show this view?
7. How is wanting equal rights different from wanting to be the same?

C

A cartoon from Punch, *1911.*

 © Folens.

Different Views 2

Background

There were many different views about the **suffragette** campaign.

Key Words

militant
suffragette

D

Alice Meynell, poet and suffragette (1847–1922). Although she never joined the window-smashing **militants** ... her son Everard supported the extreme radical group. However, family and friends, all for the vote, were equally divided about violent tactics.

(From *Salt and Bitter and Good* by Cora Kaplan, 1975.)

E

The present militant actions are mainly due to the disregard for the claims of women.

(From a letter from the Bishop of Kensington, published in *The Daily Graphic,* 1914. He believed the suffragettes were militant because the government would not take any notice of them.)

Activities

Read sources D and E.

1. Write a list of the different views which are described.
2. How did these views help the suffragettes?
3. Were any views not helpful? Give reasons for your answer.

Look again at sources A to C (page 12), D and E.

4. Tick boxes for each source like this:

Source	Recorded at the Time	Recorded Later	For Votes for Women	Against Votes for Women	Not Sure About Votes for Women
A		✔		✔	
B					
C					
D					
E					

5. Explain what 'militant' means.
How were the actions of militant suffragettes different from those of other suffragettes?

New Tactics 1

Background

Suffragettes in prison saw themselves as political prisoners, not criminals. They wanted different treatment. Marion Wallace Dunlop made this clear in July 1909 by refusing to eat. After ninety-one hours without food the prison governor let her go. The hunger strike had become a new tactic. Refusing to eat meant release from prison.
As a result the **Home Secretary** ordered force feeding. A tube was forced into the nose and throat and liquid was poured down. It was a very painful method which could result in death, but a court case to stop the practice failed. The Lord Chief Justice ruled that the prison doctor's duty was to prevent suicide.

Key Words

Home Secretary **suffragette**

A

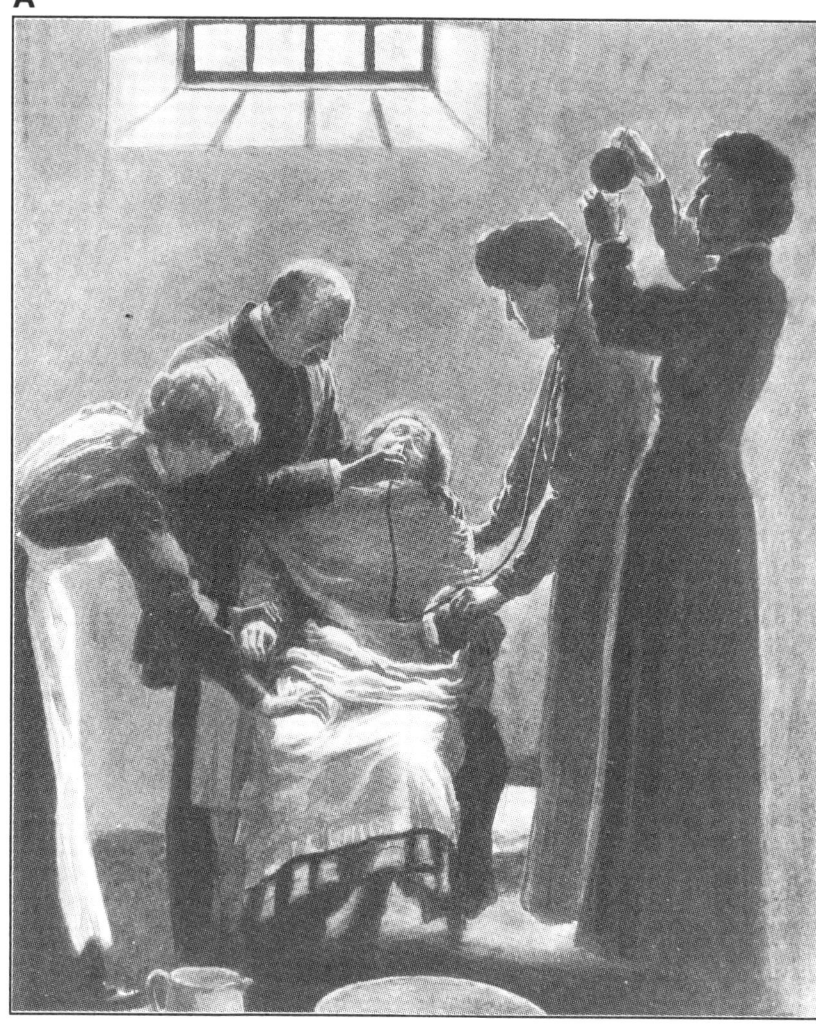

Force-feeding, 1912.

B

Canon Scott Holland declared in 1914 that "forcible feeding maddens people into criminal acts".

(From *The Suffragette Movement* by Sylvia Pankhurst, 1931.)

Activities

Look carefully at source A.

1. How does the picture show a woman being force fed?
2. Using the picture, complete a chart showing arguments for and against force feeding.

Read the background and source B.

3. What are political prisoners?
4. Should the suffragettes have been treated differently?
5. What was the government's view, as shown by the Home Secretary and the Lord Chief Justice?

 © Folens.

New Tactics 2

Background

As a result of force feeding and lack of government action, members of the **WSPU** became more and more **militant**.

Key Words

martyr
militant
suffragette
WSPU

C

Riots in the West End of London, 1912.

D

Derby Day, 4th June 1913. Emily Davison threw herself under the king's horse, Anmer, and later died. She acted without the knowledge of the WSPU.

Activities

Look at source D.

1. Choose the box which contains what you think may have been the results of Emily Davison's actions. You may choose more than one box.

make other **suffragettes** more determined	increase in public sympathy	make the government reconsider votes for women	turn Emily Davison into a suffragette **martyr**	decrease in public sympathy	make other suffragettes uneasy	have little or no long-term consequence

2. Do you think Emily Davison's death was important in gaining the vote for women? Why?

Look carefully at sources C and D.

3. How has source **D** been recorded differently from source **C**?
4. Which source is the more reliable in telling what happened? Why?
5. Talk about the advantages and disadvantages of using photographs as historical sources.

Cat and Mouse

Background

In spring 1913 the government passed the Temporary Discharge for Ill-Health Act. This meant that **suffragettes** on hunger strike would be freed, then arrested again when they were fit. The government wanted no deaths in prison. The Act became known as the Cat and Mouse Act.

Key Word

suffragette

Activities

Read the background carefully.

1. Think about how a cat plays with a mouse it catches. Why was the Act called the Cat and Mouse Act?
2. Talk about why the government wanted to avoid deaths in prison.
3. With a partner, compile a list of tactics (violent and non-violent) used by the suffragettes. Ask members of your class which tactics would have:
   - attracted public attention
   - gained public sympathy
   - lost public sympathy
   - caused the government the greatest problems.
4. Make a database of your findings. What conclusions can you draw?

Look at the poster.

5. What message does the poster give?
6. Do you think it is successful? Explain your view.
7. In what way does the poster express:
   - a fact
   - a point of view?

   Use a chart like this to list your answers.

Fact	Point of View

Suffragette election poster, 1914.

Find Out

1. Find out what happened to the Cat and Mouse Act.
2. Do you think it made things easier or more difficult for the suffragettes? Explain why.

 © Folens.

Women and War

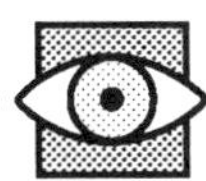

Background

In August 1914 the First World War began. **Suffragettes** in prison were released. Violent campaigning stopped. When men went to fight in the war, women did their jobs. After the war ended in 1918 a **Bill** was passed which gave the vote to women aged over thirty.
During the war many men died, so at the end of the war women outnumbered men. The men who survived returned to their old jobs. Most women were forced into the poorest work again.

Key Words

Bill **suffragette**

Activities

Read the background carefully.

1. Why were some women given the vote in 1918?
2. Why do you think only women over thirty were given the vote at this time?
3. How important was the war in gaining votes for women? Give reasons for your answer.

Look at A.

4. What are the main differences between the jobs women did before and during the war?
5. Why did this change take place?
6. Did the change last? How do you know?
7. How might the war have changed people's attitudes to women for the better?

Read source B.

8. What does this mean?
9. What does this tell you about the long-term results of the suffragettes' actions?

Find Out

Are women's rights still important today? Give reasons for your answer.

A ***Women at work before 1914 ...***

cook

scullery maid

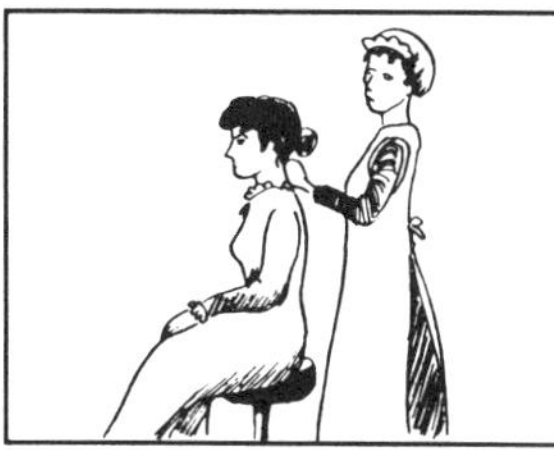

lady's maid

factory worker

... and 1914 – 1918.

driver

land army worker

policewoman

ammunition worker

B

We have an Equal Pay Act but we don't have equal pay.

(From *Women's Rights: A Practical Guide* by Anna Coote and Tessa Gill, 1974.)

Greater Democracy

Background

By 1928 all men and women over the age of twenty-one had been given the right to vote. Almost one hundred years of **reforms** had led to **democracy** in Britain.

Throughout the nineteenth century there was growing concern about the poor, the sick and the old. More working people wanted a say in the running of the country.

There was also growing tension between the **House of Lords** and the **House of Commons**. The Lords wished to keep things as they were. So did the **Conservative Party** in the House of Commons.

The **Liberal Party** and the new **Labour Party** wanted change. They felt the House of Lords and the Conservatives were not willing to help ordinary people.

A

A photograph taken in 1904.

B

Who could vote and when

Rich **middle-class** men.	1832
Male householders in towns.	1867
Male agricultural workers.	1884
Women over 30.	1918
All men and women over 21.	1928

Key Words

Conservative Party
Commons (House of)
democracy
Labour Party
Law Lord
Liberal Party
Lords (House of)
middle class
peer
reform

Activities

Look carefully at this chart.

House of Commons	House of Lords
About 650 Members of Parliament (MPs) elected by people. (The exact number of MPs changes from time to time.)	Hereditary **peers** (people who inherited a title). Life peers (people who were given a title). **Law Lords** (top judges). Archbishops. Bishops. (Nobody elected by the people.)

1. Talk about the differences between the House of Lords and the House of Commons.

Read the background.

2. Why was it felt the Lords did not want to help ordinary people?

Look carefully at source A.

3. How do the boys earn their living?
4. Are they aware of the photographer?
5. Do you think they posed for this photograph?
6. Does this affect the reliability of the source? What other information will help you decide?
7. How might the reforms in **B** have created better conditions for street children?

© Folens.

The Commons Versus the Lords

Background

In 1900 the two main political parties were the **Conservatives (Tories)** and the **Liberals**. The Conservatives had held power for the longest and had many supporters in the **House of Lords**. However, in 1906 the Liberals won the **election**. Lloyd George, the **Chancellor of the Exchequer**, introduced new social **reforms** and new taxes to pay for them. The Lords rejected these plans and so another election was called. The Liberals won again but with a tiny **majority**. They decided that the power of the Lords would have to be limited if any laws were going to be passed. To do this the Parliament **Bill** was introduced.

Key Words

Bill
Chancellor
Conservative Party
election
Liberal Party
Lords (House of)
majority
peer
reform
Tory
veto

A

*The prime minister asked the king to create Liberal **peers** in the House of Lords.*

The king said the people must decide. An election was called.

The Liberals won again.

*The Lords had their power of **veto** reduced. The Parliament Bill was law.*

Activities

Look at the background and A.

1. How could the Parliament Bill become law if it had to go through the House of Lords?

Look at the background and B.

2. How were the reforms paid for?
3. Why did the Liberals want to reduce the power of the Lords?
4. List two results of the Liberals gaining power.

Find Out

1. Find out more about the main political views of the Liberals and Tories in 1906.
2. Draw a chart showing their different views.

B Social reforms created:

old age pensions

unemployment benefits

health insurance

free school meals

Poverty and Hardship 1

Background

The nineteenth century **Reform** Acts did little to help the poor. Poverty was not seen as Parliament's concern. It was believed that if you worked hard you would be rewarded. If you were poor it was your own fault. In fact, better off people did not believe conditions were as bad as they were for the **working class**.

Key Words

reform
working class

Activities

Look at source A.
When artists paint pictures they choose to show what they think is important. A painting is an artist's *interpretation* of a person, place or event.

1. Make a list of words which describe these people.
2. What do you think was the artist's view of work and working people?

Look at source B.

3. How are the people in this picture different from those in source **A**? Look carefully at their surroundings and what they are doing.

A

A detail from Work by Ford Madox Brown. Painted between 1852 and 1865.

B

A farm labourer's home, 1862.

 © Folens.

Poverty and Hardship 2

Background

Working-class children often lived in poor conditions and suffered great hardship because of poverty.

Key Word

working class

C

A still from a film version of Oliver Twist *by Charles Dickens.*

D

Henry Mayhew claimed his book *London Labour and the London Poor* (1862) was 'the history of a people from the lips of the people themselves'. Here is an extract from his chapter about a watercress girl.

"I go about the streets with water-cress, crying, 'Four bunches a penny water-cress' ... I bear the cold – you must; so I put my hands under my shawl, though it hurts 'em to take hold of the cress, especially when I wash 'em ... All the money I earn I put in a club and draw out to buy clothes with. It's better than spending it on sweets, for them as has a living to earn. Besides it's like a child to care for sugar-sticks, and not like one who's got a living to earn. I ain't a child, and I shan't be a woman till I'm twenty but I'm past eight, I am."

Activities

Look closely at the film still C.

1. How does this source show poverty?
2. How is it similar to source **B** (page 20)?
3. In your view which source shows poverty and hardship more accurately, **B** or **C**?
4. Which of these sources is the more important? Why?

Read source D carefully.

5. Describe the watercress girl.
6. Write three ways in which source **D** shows poverty.
7. Why do you think Henry Mayhew thought it was important to record the history of the people from the words of the people?

The Rise of Socialism

Background

Towards the end of the nineteenth century a new view of society began to emerge. Karl Marx believed that a country's wealth was created by the workers. The work they did created money for the rich people who employed them but paid them poorly. The goods they made were sold for a profit and the rich people kept most of it. This was how **capitalism** worked.
In 1892 two members of the Independent Labour Party (ILP), Keir Hardie and John Burns, became **MPs**. They followed Karl Marx's ideas of **socialism**. By 1906 there were fifty-three MPs from different Labour groups. They were to form the basis of the present-day **Labour Party**.

CAPITAL AND LABOUR.

A cartoon from Punch, *1843.*

Key Words

capitalism
Communism
immigrant
Labour Party
MP
socialism

Activities

Look at the cartoon.

1. Describe what is happening in the cartoon.
2. Who are the rich?
3. Who are the workers?
4. What position does the Black person hold?
5. How is this cartoon influenced by Karl Marx's ideas? Read the background to help you.

Find Out

1. Many **immigrants** lived in Britain in the nineteenth century. Find books or other sources which mention them. Write about a day in the life of someone living in one of these communities.
2. Find out more about Karl Marx. Explain his ideas of **Communism**.

 © Folens.

Divide and Fall

Background

In the first half of the twentieth century, the new **Labour Party** grew and the **Liberals** lost support. Quarrels split the Liberal Party. Lloyd George wanted to raise taxes to pay for social **reforms**, but not everyone agreed with him. Many Liberals did not want to take Britain to war in 1914. In 1916 Lloyd George formed a pact with the **Conservatives** and became the new prime minister of a **coalition** government. After the First World War there was high unemployment. Lloyd George became more and more unpopular. In the 1922 **election** the Conservatives won. The Liberals have never been in power since.

Key Words

coalition	**Labour Party**
Conservative Party	**Liberal Party**
election	**reform**

Activities

Look at source A.

1. Which person is Lloyd George?
2. Who is the other person?
3. Why is the poster called 'The Dawn of Hope'?
4. In what ways does it *not* show some Liberal MPs' views? Read the background to help you.

Look at source B.

5. What did Lloyd George want to take from people who were better off? Why?
6. What view of Lloyd George does this cartoon give?
7. Why might some Liberals have agreed with this view of him? Read the background again to help you.

Look at all the information on this page.

8. Talk about these two views of Lloyd George.

A

THE DAWN OF HOPE.

Mr. LLOYD GEORGE'S National Health Insurance Bill provides for the insurance of the Worker in case of Sickness.

Support the Liberal Government
in their policy of
SOCIAL REFORM.

A government poster, 1911.

B

A cartoon from Punch, *1909.*
Lloyd George is the giant. Hiding from him is a member of the wealthy class.

Right, Left and In-Between

Background

After the **Liberals** lost support, the two main **political parties** were **Conservative** and **Labour**. Conservatives are the **right wing** of politics, Labour are the **left wing**. This is called a **two-party system**, where two parties hold very different views. It does not allow much room for a third party, which can be seen as in between. There have been governments in which all three parties have united in times of crisis, such as war. These are called **coalition** governments. However, they do not usually work well in peace time.

Key Words

coalition
Commons (House of)
Conservative Party
Labour Party
left wing
Liberal Party
political party
right wing
two-party system

A

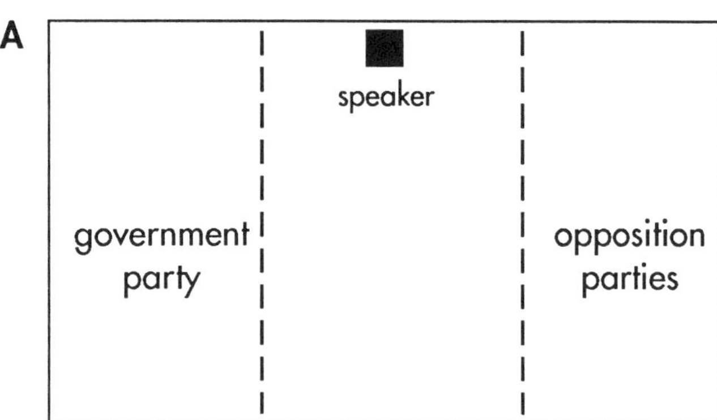

The ***House of Commons***

B

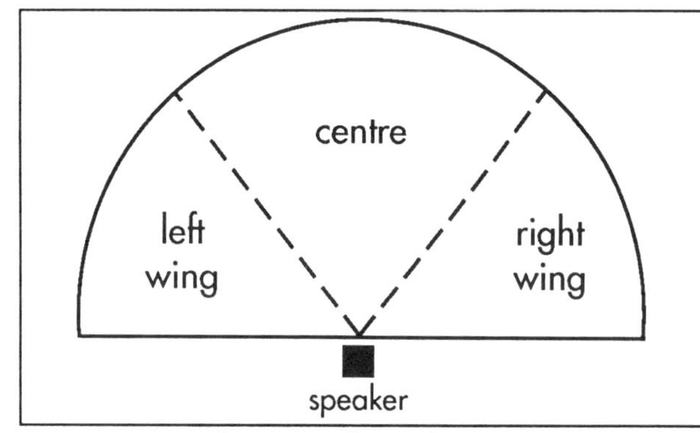

The French Parliament

C

A cartoon from Punch, *1931. Ramsay Macdonald was the head of a coalition government.*

Activities

Look carefully at A and B.

1. How is the design of **A** different from that of **B**?
2. How does design **A** encourage a two-party system in Britain?

Look at the cartoon C.

3. What does it show Ramsay Macdonald doing?
4. Why are the jars different sizes? What do the labels mean?
5. Explain what you think the message of the cartoon is.

Find Out

1. What would a government poster in favour of a coalition say? Use this sheet to help you.
2. Do some research into the advantages and disadvantages of coalition governments.

 © Folens.

The 1945 Election

Background

Between 1918 and 1939 Britain went through major difficulties. The **Depression** brought high unemployment and great hardship. The Second World War caused much suffering. In 1942 the **Beveridge Report** showed how living conditions could be improved. After the war ended, in the run up to the 1945 **election** the **Labour Party** promised to put the Beveridge Report into practice. Winston Churchill and his coalition government had led the country to victory. He and the **Conservatives** expected to win the election, but Labour won with a massive **majority**.

Key Words

Beveridge Report
Conservative Party
Depression
election
Labour Party
majority

A

A cartoon by David Low, 1945.

B

> During the Second World War we realised that we must go forward and not back, because the times between the wars were not good.
>
> (From *Power and Influence* by William Beveridge.)

Activities

Look at the cartoon carefully.

1. Who is the main figure meant to be?
2. Where is he going?
3. Who are the others?
4. How does the cartoon show only one point of view?

Look at source B.

5. What did Beveridge mean when he wrote 'we must go forward and not back'?
6. What does the cartoon show happening to people who did not agree?
7. Which source is more reliable, **A** or **B**? Why?
8. Does this make it more useful to historians?

Find Out

Find out more about the reasons for Labour's election victory in 1945. Write a list of as many reasons as you can.

Post-War Change

Background

By 1950 the **Beveridge Report** was in practice. Throughout the 1950s and 1960s, under both **Labour** and **Conservative** governments, people wanted the right to a healthy life, decent housing and free education. **Working-class** people began to own cars, televisions, refrigerators and other goods. There seemed to be fewer differences between the two main **political parties**. Harold Macmillan, the Conservative Prime Minister between 1957 and 1963, was called a **Tory Socialist**. The Labour government became more conservative between 1964 and 1970. In the 1970 **election** fewer people voted. Perhaps they felt there was not much to choose between the two parties. However, when the Conservatives won the 1970 election they became more **right wing**. When Margaret Thatcher became leader in 1975 the change towards right-wing ideas was complete.

A cartoon from The Spectator, *1959, showing Harold Macmillan after winning the election.*

Key Words

Beveridge Report
Conservative Party
election
Labour Party
political party
right wing
Tory Socialist
working class

Find Out

1. Find out more about how the nation's attitude to poverty changed between 1900 and 1950.
2. How quick was the change?

Activities

Study the cartoon.

1. What does this cartoon suggest won the election for Macmillan?

Read the background, then look at the cartoon again.

2. In what way is it similar to the background?
3. Make a chart to list three facts and three opinions from the background and the cartoon.
4. Interview two adults who remember the 1950s, 1960s and 1970s.
   Find out:
   - what life was like at the time
   - how Labour and Conservative were different
   - how attitudes to poverty were changing.

   Draw a chart to display your findings.

 © Folens.

What is Democracy?

Background

Democracy means 'rule by the people'. British democracy has developed over hundreds of years. Only in the last thirty years have all adults over eighteen years old gained the right to decide who governs them. Britain is a **representative** democracy. Any citizen aged over twenty-one can stand for **election** and become an **MP**. General elections must be held at least every five years.

Key Words

candidate
democracy
election
Member of Parliament
policy
political party
representative

1.

Candidates stand for election.

2.

Conservative
Labour
Liberal Democrats

Most belong to ***political parties*** *and stand for their* ***policies****.*

3.

People vote for one candidate.

4.

The candidate with the most votes wins.

5.

He or she becomes a Member of Parliament (MP).

6.

MPs make decisions on behalf of the people.

Activity

Use this questionnaire to find out about young people's voting habits.

Question In a general election would you vote for...	**Number of People** Use tally marks to show how many people choose each option, e.g. 𝍸 = 5.	**Totals**
The best candidate		
The best policies		
The best leader		
The party my family has always voted for		
Won't vote		

1. Ask at least twenty people between the ages of eighteen and twenty.
2. Add your findings to a partner's.
3. Make a database of both your findings.
4. What was your most important finding?

Find Out

1. When did the voting age become eighteen?
2. Which three groups do not have the right to vote?

Constitutions and Rights 1

Background

A **constitution** is a set of rules by which a country is governed. The American constitution is a written statement. In Britain there is no written statement of the constitution. The law is guided by what has happened in the past or what usually happens. This is called 'custom and practice'. There are three main parts to the government in Britain.

Key Words

cabinet
Commons (House of)
constitution
executive
judiciary
legislature
Lords (House of)
policy

The **Executive**

*The prime minister and the **cabinet** (other chief ministers). They make **policies**.*

The **Legislature**

*The **House of Commons** and the **House of Lords**. They approve government policies and pass laws.*

The **Judiciary**

The Law Courts. They decide what the law means.

Some Common Rights

An important part of a constitution is the rights it gives to its citizens. In Britain these rights include:

- the right to vote
- freedom of speech
- the right to a fair trial
- the right to be free from wrongful arrest
- the right to form a trade union
- the right to be free from discrimination on the grounds of race, gender or religion.

 © Folens.

Constitutions and Rights 2

Background

The rights of citizens are an important part of a **constitution**. The rights of the people of Britain have developed over hundreds of years. Sometimes arguments about a person's rights have to be settled by the courts.

Key Word

constitution

Twelve-year-old Theresa Bennett had no choice about joining Muskham United, her local football club. The Nottingham Football Association and the Football Association would not let her join because she was a girl – and she sued them. In the Appeal Court, Lord Denning ruled that it made no difference whether she was as good as any boy of her age. The Sex Discrimination Act did not include "any sport ... where the physical strength, stamina or physique of the average woman puts her at a disadvantage to the average man". In other words, Ms Bennett was not judged on her own football skills, as any boy would have been, but by the average football skills of all women.

(An account of *Bennett versus the Football Association* (1978), from *Sweet Freedom* by Anna Coote and Beatrix Campbell, 1982.)

Activities

Read the source carefully.

1. What right did Theresa Bennett feel she was being denied? Check the 'Common Rights' list.
2. Did she win or lose her case?
3. Do you think the result was fair?
4. What is the authors' view?
5. Is the authors' view the same or different from Lord Denning's decision? Give reasons for your answer.
6. Interview two PE teachers, a man and a woman. Ask if they feel Theresa Bennett was dealt with fairly.
7. Write an account of their opinions.
8. Conduct a survey in your class to find out who agrees that Theresa Bennett should have been allowed to join the football club, and who disagrees.
9. Present your results in the form of a graph or a chart.

Find Out

Do some research and write a list of the rights which are most important to people today.

Proportional Representation

Background

The place an **MP** represents is called a **constituency**. In Britain there is one MP for each constituency. The **candidate** with the most votes in the constituency is **elected**. The system is called **first past the post**.
In **Eire** the voting system is called **proportional representation** (**PR**). There are many complicated PR systems. The diagram below shows very simply what PR means.

Key Words

candidate
constituency
Eire
election
first past the post
MP
PR

There are three candidates and two seats to be won.
300 people have voted, putting each candidate in order of preference.
A candidate must get 101 votes to win because 300 votes divided by three candidates = 100.

Nora Gibbons got

Mary O'Donovan got

Desmond McNeil got

Nora Gibbons is the first choice of 130 people, so she will be elected.
She needs only 101 votes to win. She has twenty-nine votes spare, which are then shared out.

Desmond McNeil now has

Mary O'Donovan now has

Desmond McNeil is second choice of twenty-two people, so he gets these votes.
Mary O'Donovan is second choice of seven people, so she gets these votes.
So Nora Gibbons and Desmond McNeil are elected.

Activities

1. Read these views. Which view do you agree with? Discuss your opinions with a partner.

I like PR. It's more democratic. Under first past the post the party I voted for got millions of votes but often came second or third. It ended up with a lot fewer MPs.

I don't like PR. There are too many MPs from small parties. There are no clear cut policies. Nothing gets done. We end up with a weak government.

2. Interview six people to find out what they think about PR and first past the post. Draw a chart to show the advantages and disadvantages of each system.

 © Folens.

The Presidential System

Background

The **USA** has a presidential system of government which is different from a parliamentary system.

A

The Presidential System	The Parliamentary System
President	Prime Minister
• Elected by the people	• Leader of the party, elected by the party
• Cannot hold office in Congress	• A member of the House of Commons
• Makes policy	• Makes policy with the Cabinet
• Head of Cabinet	• Head of Cabinet

Congress has two Houses. Congress can change government policy (make amendments). Both Houses can make laws. Each House is checked by the other. There is also the Supreme Court.

The Senate (Upper House)	The House of Representatives (Lower House)	The Supreme Court
Senators are elected by each State. They are in power for six years.	*Each American State elects Representatives who remain in power for two years.*	*Judges are appointed by the President to decide the meaning of the law.*

Key Words

Congress
policy
USA

Activities

Look at source A.

1. List three differences between presidential and parliamentary systems.

Look at source B.

2. Describe what is happening in the cartoon.
3. In what way does the cartoon show only one point of view?
4. Does this make it less useful as a source or not? Give reasons.

B

"JUMP!"

A cartoon from Punch, *1974.*
In 1974 President Nixon resigned after the Watergate scandal. He was threatened with impeachment – being charged with abusing his position. The scandal upset the American people's trust in the presidency.

The One-Party System

Background

The **USSR** (Union of Soviet Socialist Republics) was the largest **one-party** state.
The **Communist Party** was in control. There were no other official **political parties**.

Key Words

candidate
Communist
Communist Party
constituency
democracy
elections
executive
legislature
one-party system
policy
Politburo
political parties
two-party system
USSR

The USSR was controlled by the CPSU (Communist Party of the Soviet Union).
This was how the one-party system worked.

CPSU

The General Secretary (leader) headed members of the ***Politburo****.*

The **Executive**

Council of ministers who carried out CPSU ***policies****.*

The **Legislature** (Supreme Soviet)

Soviet of the Union (650–700 members)

Soviet of Nationalities (650–700 members)

They accepted CPSU policies.

Praesidium

Some members of the Supreme Soviet who passed laws.

During national **elections** only one person chosen by the CPSU could stand in each **constituency**. The people could not choose between one **candidate** and another.

Activities

1. What is the most important difference between a one-party system and a **two-party system**? Check your glossary to help you.
2. Some **Communist** countries called themselves 'one-party **democracies**'. Why?

 © Folens.

How Democratic is Democracy?

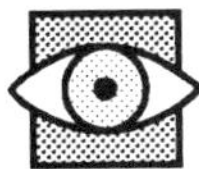

Background

Democracy means 'rule by the people', but not everyone is satisfied by the way the democratic system works.

Key Words

democracy
media
MP
multi-racial
Parliament
policy
political party

A

Here are some of the main worries people have about democracy.

- **MPs** do not always represent what the people want.
- **Parliament** does not represent a **multi-racial** society.
- There are too few women MPs.
- **Policies** and laws have different effects on the rich and the poor.
- The **media** (television, radio and the press) is controlled by powerful people. They are biased towards one political party.

Activities

Look at A.

1. Which two worries listed do you think are the most important? Explain why.
2. Explain what 'bias' means.

Look at the cartoon.

2. Why are the media referred to as 'Mafia Incorporated'?
3. What power does this cartoon suggest the speaker has?
4. Do you think the cartoon itself is biased against the media? Give reasons.
5. Choose one of the worries from **A**. How would you show it in a cartoon or poster?

B

Agreed then, lads – two days of mild Ted-bashing, then all back to Wedgewood Benn again!

A cartoon from the Evening Standard, 1972.
'Ted' is Edward Heath, Conservative Prime Minister 1970–1974.
'Wedgewood Benn' is Tony Benn, a Labour MP.

Conflict in Ireland

Background

In 1969 British soldiers were sent to Northern Ireland to control the violence which had broken out there. They have been there ever since. Conflict in Northern Ireland is not new. In 1921 the south (now called **Eire**) became a separate state. Six counties in the north (**Ulster**) remained part of Britain. Many people are unhappy with this arrangement. The **Republicans** want a united Ireland. The **Unionists** want to remain under British rule. No solution has yet been found.

Key Words

Catholic
Commons (House of)
Eire
IRA
Loyalist
MP
Nationalist
paramilitary
Protestant
Republican
Sinn Fein
Ulster
Unionist

A

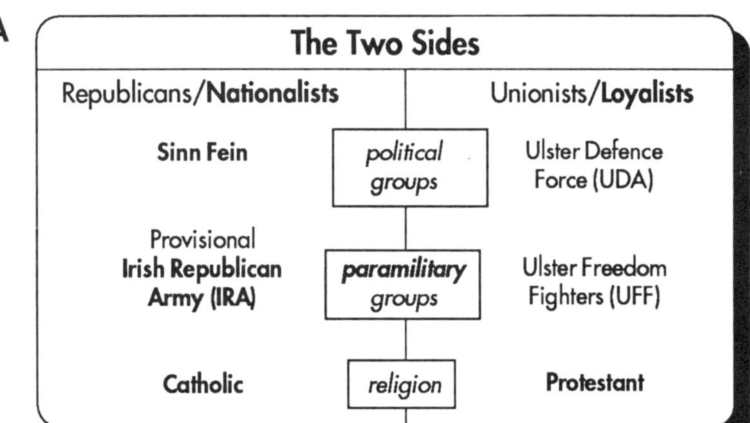

B

Ulster
Northern Ireland's
Six Counties

C

In 1969 twenty-one year old Bernadette Devlin became an independent **MP** for Northern Ireland. When she entered the **Commons** she brought grim warnings ... but London never really bothered with her remarks. It was thought ... rather super that modern youth should have its say, though not many actually considered what she was saying.

(From a report by Ian Lyon in the *Illustrated London News*, August 1969.)

Activities

Read source C.

1. What warnings of trouble do you think Bernadette Devlin gave? Read the background to help you.
2. How do **A** and **B** support her view?
3. What attitude do you think other MPs had towards her?
4. Ask three adults if they agree with Bernadette Devlin's views. Write a summary of their views.

Find Out

Look at A.

1. Find out why the name Sinn Fein was chosen for a Republican political group.
2. Why were the other names chosen?

 © Folens.

Catholics and Protestants

Background

Some people believe that the problems of Northern Ireland are mainly to do with religion. They believe that it is a **sectarian** conflict between **Catholics** and **Protestants**. This is only a small part of the story. The problems are not so much to do with a difference of religion itself but with the way Catholics and Protestants have been treated.
When England took Ireland by force in the seventeenth century, large numbers of Protestants settled there. Then the Protestant William of Orange defeated the Catholic King James II at the Battle of the Boyne in 1690. Under his reign anti-Catholic laws were passed in Ireland and many Catholics saw Protestants as representing the enemy, England.

A

"The Irish fighting amongst themselves again. Will they never settle their age-old religious problems?"

(Gerry Fitt (MP) describing the English view of the 'Irish problem', 1970.)

B

Home rule means Rome rule.

(A popular saying in 1914. Rome refers to Catholics.)

C

A cartoon from a history book, 1991.

Activities

Read source A.

1. How has Gerry Fitt described the 'English view of the Irish problem'?
2. Do you think he was right to view the English in this way?
3. Is he biased? Give reasons for your answer.

Read source B.

4. Who would have said this?
5. What opinion does this show?
6. Does that make it an unreliable source? Why?

Look at source C.

7. What opinion does this cartoon show?
8. In what way is this source different from sources **A** and **B**?

Key Words

Catholic
Protestant
sectarian

Find Out

1. Find out more about the problems in Ireland since 1969.
2. Explain how the Irish problem is not only a religious one.

Home Rule and the Easter Rising

Background

Home Rule means partial **self-government** for Ireland. It has been discussed many times. In 1912 a new **Bill** for home rule was presented to the **House of Commons**. The **Unionists** fiercely objected. They formed their own army, the Ulster Volunteer Force (UVF), while the **Nationalists** formed the Irish Volunteers. It seemed as though civil war would break out. Then in 1914 the First World War began. Home rule was postponed.
One group of **Republicans** wanted full **independence**. In Easter 1916, Patrick Pearse, James Connelly and their supporters attempted an uprising, although they knew they would probably fail. Fighting against British troops continued for a week until the rebels finally gave in. They were executed by firing squad soon after.

A

Unionist poster, 1914.

Key Words

Bill
Commons (House of)
Easter Rising
Home Rule
independence
Nationalist
Republican
self-government
Unionist

B

> Ulster will fight,
> And Ulster will be right.
>
> (Randolph Churchill, who opposed home rule, 1886.)

C

Executions of Irish republicans by British troops following the ***Easter Rising****, 1916.*

Activities

Look carefully at sources A and B.

1. Who would have made the poster? Why?
2. Why has the figure been 'deserted'?
3. What does source **B** have in common with source **A**? List two points.

Look at source C.

4. What is happening in this painting?
5. What is the figure on the left doing?
6. Give one possible long-term consequence of the Easter Rising. Why do you think this?

 © Folens.

Partition

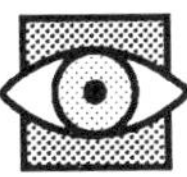

Background

By 1918 support for the **Republicans** in Ireland had grown. In the **election Sinn Fein** won over seventy places in **Parliament**. By 1919 the **paramilitary Irish Republican Army (IRA)** had formed. The British felt there would never be peace without **independence**. However, complete independence would anger the **Unionists**. Lloyd George, the Prime Minister, decided to **partition** the country. The Unionists would keep Ulster. The rest of Ireland would become the **Irish Free State**.
Both sides signed the British **treaty** in 1921. The Unionists were afraid the whole country might become independent if they did not sign. The Republicans felt that partition need only be temporary. But partition was not at all acceptable to some Republicans. Michael Collins, who had signed the treaty, was **assassinated** in 1922.

The Lord Mayor of Cork and member of the IRA died on hunger strike in 1920. On his coffin was written 'Murdered by the Foreigner'.

Key Words

assassinate
election
independence
IRA
Irish Free State
paramilitary
Parliament
partition
Republicans
Sinn Fein
treaty
Unionist

Find Out

Find out more about the partition of Ireland.
1. Write a list of the consequences.
2. What consequences are important today?

Activities

Read the background carefully.
1. List three reasons why the British felt peace in Ireland would be hard to achieve.

Look at the picture.
2. Why do you think the coffin is open?
3. How might the mayor's death have helped the Republicans?
4. What does the writing on the coffin mean?
5. Why do you think the photographer chose to take this picture? Give two reasons.

Civil Rights

Background

Violence in Northern Ireland increased after 1921. The Special Powers **Act** was introduced. There was great mistrust between the **Protestant** and **Catholic** communities. Protestants wanted full control, believing that the Catholic **minority** would not be loyal to **Ulster**. The voting system was changed. **Proportional Representation (PR)** was dropped. This had allowed Catholics some **MPs**. Now fewer Catholic MPs were in **Parliament**. Catholics felt they were being **discriminated** against. By the 1960s a strong **civil rights** movement had grown.

Key Words

Act
Catholic
civil rights
discrimination
MP
minority
Parliament
PR
Protestant
Ulster

A

A civil rights march, 1969.

Activities

Look at source A.

1. Are these Catholics or Protestants marching?
2. Give two reasons why they are marching.

Read the background and look at B.

3. Is **B** fact or opinion?
4. Why might Catholics suffer more ill treatment under this Act than Protestants?
5. Which is more useful as a historical source, **A** or **B**? Give reasons for your answer.
6. Why is PR a better voting system for Catholics?

B

The Special Powers Act 1922 gave the police greater powers, including:

- the power to arrest and hold people without trial
- the power to search houses without special permission.

 © Folens.

Ireland's Future

Background

In January 1972, thirteen people in Belfast were killed by British soldiers during a **civil rights** march on 'Bloody Sunday'. In revenge the **IRA** killed five people with a bomb at Aldershot army barracks. In March 1972 Britain decided to rule directly from London. The government in Northern Ireland was disbanded. Most people in Northern Ireland want peace, but Ireland's history makes this difficult. Many **Protestants** feel that in a united Ireland they would suffer **discrimination** because they would be the **minority**. Nor do they like the **Catholic** Church. They fear talks between **Eire** and Britain. Meanwhile the conflict continues.

Key Words

Catholic
civil rights
discrimination
Eire
IRA
minority
Protestant

A

A British soldier on guard in Belfast, 1969.

B

A bomb-thrower shot by a soldier, 1921.

C

Rioting in Derry, 1970

Activities

Look at sources A, B and C.

1. Choose one picture and make two posters:
   - a civil rights poster
   - a British army recruiting poster.
2. Write a suitable caption for each one.
3. Source **B** was recorded fifty years before sources **A** and **C**. What does this suggest about how the conflict has been dealt with?
4. Has anything been achieved in the years between these photographs?

Find Out

There are a number of options for the future of Northen Ireland:

- unite Ireland (make Northern Ireland and Eire one country)
- make Northern Ireland a separate country
- set up a new government in Northern Ireland but retain it as part of Britain.

Discuss these suggestions with your teacher and write an account of why they would or would not work.

The Growth of Trade Unions

Background

Throughout history, workers' protest groups have tried to improve working conditions. As factories grew and large numbers of workers came together so **trade unions** grew. The **Trades Union Congress (TUC)** is an association of trade unions formed in 1868.
At first the better paid craftsmen did not feel it was their duty to support the unskilled workers, who formed their own unions at the end of the nineteeth century after several successful strikes. These 'new' unions were strongly influenced by **socialism**. They soon formed links with the **Labour Party**. The first two Labour **MP**s, Kier Hardie and John Burns of the Independent Labour Party (ILP), spoke for these working men.

A

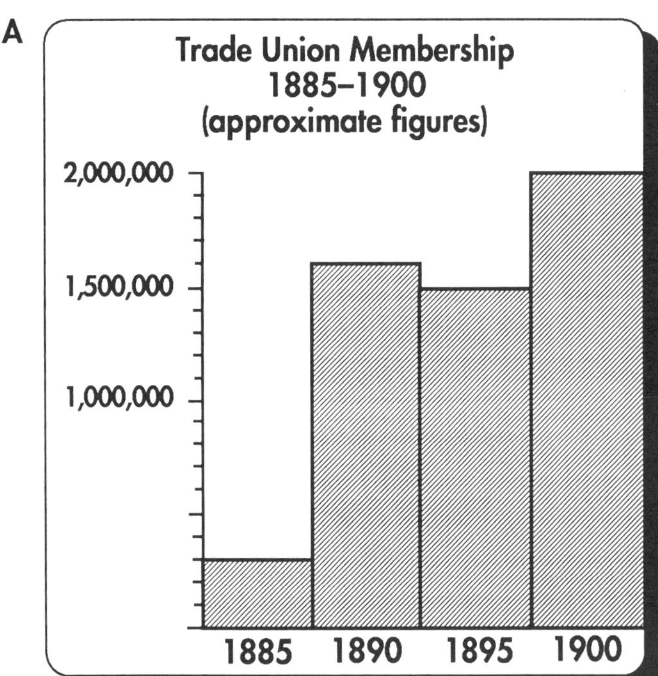

Key Words

Labour Party
MP
socialism
trade unions
TUC

B

Successful Strikes by Unskilled Workers	
Bryant & May Match Girls	1888
London Dockers	1889
Gas Workers	1889

Activities

Look at A and B.

1. Give one reason why union membership increased so much between 1885 and 1890.
2. There were other reasons for the increase in membership. Find out more about trade unions at this time and list these reasons.

Look at source C.

3. What does it tell you about the aims of the ILP?
4. What do you think the figure represents?
5. What was the connection between the 'new' unions and the ILP? Read the background.

C

An ILP election poster, 1895.

 © Folens.

The General Strike

Background

Between 1918 and 1939 unemployment was high and pay was low. In 1925 mine owners cut miners' wages and made the working day longer. The **Trades Union Congress (TUC)** threatened to take action. In 1926 a **General Strike** was called. About three million workers supported the miners. The government kept basic goods available with the help of the army, police and public volunteers. Neither the government nor the TUC wanted the situation to get worse. They were afraid of violence and even revolution. After discussions the TUC called off the strike. The miners felt betrayed. Their action continued for another seven months.

Key Words

General Strike
TUC

A

Not a penny off the pay
Not a minute on the day.

(A popular saying by A.J. Cook, 1926.)

B

Volunteers at work during the General Strike, 1926. Artist's impression, 1994.

C

The New Leader

The Shadow of Hunger

Cover of The New Leader *(a journal of the Independent Labour Party), June 1926.*

Activities

Look at source A.

1. Explain what this saying means.
2. Who would have chanted this?

Look at source B.

3. What effect did volunteers have on the strike?
4. Should they have done the strikers' work? Give reasons for your answer.

Look at source C.

5. Explain who the people are.
6. What is the shadow meant to be?
7. List three ways in which this source is similar to source **A**.
8. Source **B** is an artist's impression, drawn seventy years after the event. Does this make it a less important source than **A** and **C**? Give reasons for your answer.

Unions and the State: the 1970s

Background

Trade union membership grew steadily after 1945. By 1960 about half the working population were members of a trade union. During the 1960s and the 1970s union action increased. In 1973 miners' industrial action cut power supplies. Without gas and electricity, industries could not operate. This caused a three-day working week and the crisis helped to bring about an **election** in 1974.

Key Words

election
trade union

Activities

Look at source A.

1. How are the trade unions presented?
2. What are they going to do?
3. Explain why:
   - the house is number ten
   - there are sharks in the water
   - there is a poster saying 'Eat, drink and be merry'.

Look at source B.

4. Who is the gangster meant to be?
5. How is the worker presented?
6. Talk about two views of trade unions presented in sources **A** and **B**.

A

These cartoons from Punch *show different attitudes to unions, employers and the government in 1974.*

B

"As soon as the factory is producing cars again we're going to take you for a ride."

 © Folens.

The Beveridge Report

Background

In 1942 a committee led by William Beveridge published its report on living conditions in Britain. Beveridge said that action should be taken by the government to remove poverty. A range of **Acts** were passed following the report. These became the basis of the **Welfare State**. The right of everyone to a decent standard of living was established.

Key Words

Act
Welfare State

Activities

1. Beveridge outlined five areas of concern. Link them to their opposites.

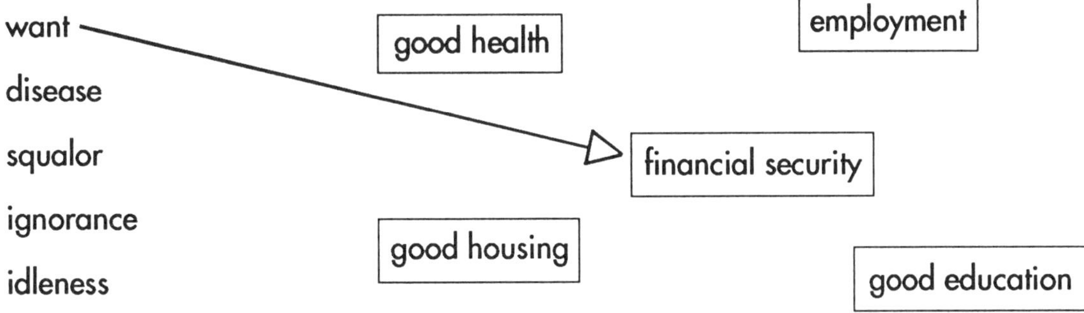

2. These are some of the Acts passed to remove poverty. Link them to their consequences.

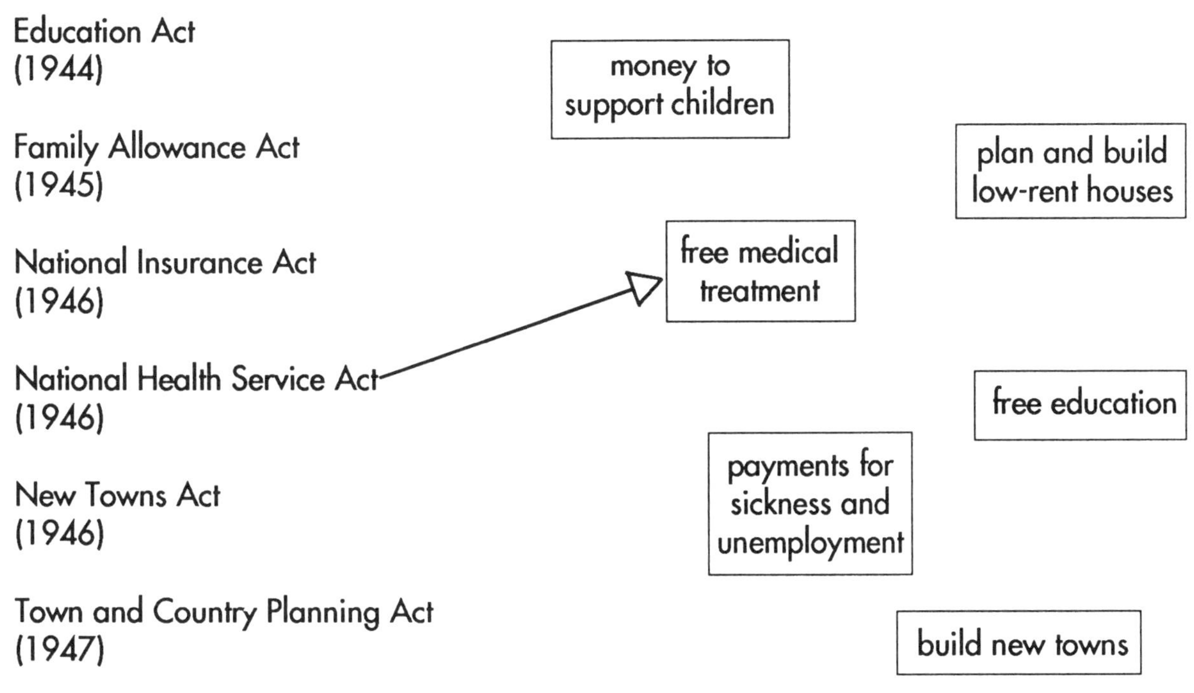

The National Health Service

Background

An important part of the **Welfare State** is the **National Health Service (NHS)**. It was set up in 1948 by the Minister for Health, Aneurin Bevan. He believed that free medical care would raise health standards.
At the time not everyone agreed with the NHS. They thought it would cost too much and people would not help themselves.

Key Words

Labour Party
NHS
Welfare State

A

In the first year the NHS cared for forty-seven and a half million patients ... It was the most important of the **Labour** government's innovations and the one which has had the deepest effect on lives and attitudes in Britain ever since. By 1950, nineteen people out of twenty were using the NHS.

(From *Great Events of the Twentieth Century*, ILN, 1989)

B

C

Cartoons from Punch, *1974.*

Activities

Read source A.
1. List two facts and two opinions from this account.
2. What view of the NHS does this source present?
3. What long-term result does it say the NHS had?

Look at sources B and C.
4. What view of the NHS does **B** present?
5. Is this view similar to or different from:
   - source **A**?
   - source **C**?
   In what way?
6. All these sources were recorded long after the NHS began. Look at sources **B** and **C** again. Then read the background. What does this tell you about people's views of the NHS?

 © Folens.

A Decent Standard of Living ?

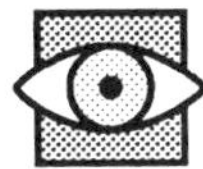

Background

The **Welfare State** was set up to help remove poverty. There are different opinions about how far it has done this and about what we understand poverty to be.

Key Word

Welfare State

A

A pensioner who cannot afford to buy a present for her grandchild is poor.

B

That's not poverty! Being poor is when you have no clothes or nowhere to live.

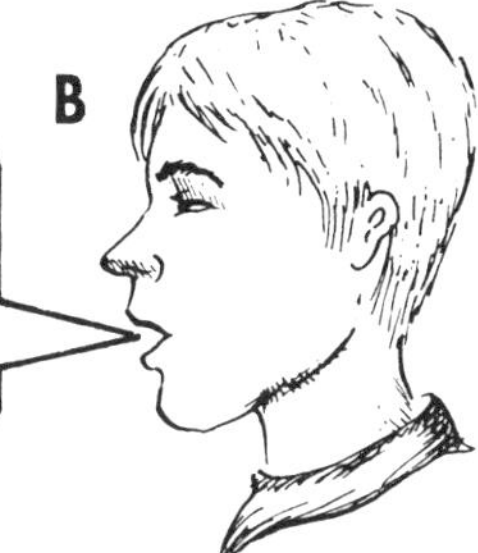

C

The Supplementary Benefit Commission* (1978) said that those who claim benefits should have enough money 'to participate in the life of the community'.

* A report which stated the basics for daily life.

D

Three boys photographed in 1900.

Activities

Read carefully opinions A and B.

1. Explain how these opinions are different.
2. Which opinion do you agree with? Why?

Read source C.

3. Explain what this source means.
4. Does this source agree with **A** or **B**? Give reasons for your answer.

Look at source D.

5. Use this photograph to make two posters about the Welfare State:
   - one to show its success
   - another to show its failure.
6. What does this tell you about the way sources can be used by historians?
7. How might a historian's opinion affect how sources are interpreted?

Find Out

1. Interview a relative or friend who remembers the Welfare State in the 1950s. Ask:
   - what changes they have seen
   - how they would describe poverty then and now
   - if they think the Welfare State has succeeded or failed.

   Compare your findings with a partner's.

2. Make a list of five points you feel are essential for a decent standard of living.

Public and Private

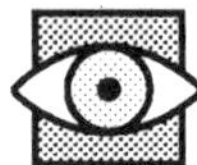

Background

In 1918 the **Labour Party** said it wanted to place the main industries such as coal mining, railways, iron and steel under government control. These industries would no longer be privately owned. They would be under public ownership. This was called **nationalisation**. By 1945 many industries had been nationalised, but in recent years there has been a move back to private ownership and away from nationalisation. This is called **privatisation**.

A

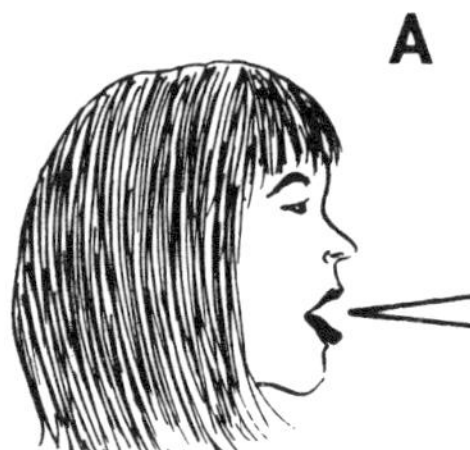

Governments must look after main industries. We all need them. I'm prepared to pay more taxes.

B

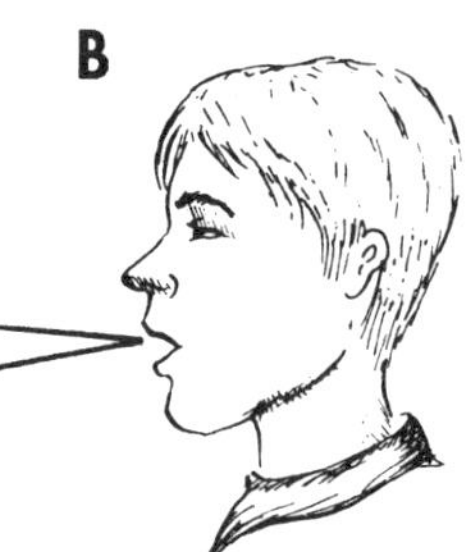

If an industry fails to make money why should I support it through my taxes? I want to keep more of my hard-earned money.

Key Words

Labour Party
nationalisation
privatisation

Activities

Read the background and opinions A and B.

1. What is nationalisation?
2. What views are expressed about nationalisation in opinions **A** and **B**?

Look at source C.

3. In what way is this poster biased?
4. Which party do you think produced it?
5. Does it support opinion **A** or **B**? Give reasons for your answer.

Find Out

Find out as much as you can about nationalisation and privatisation.
Hold a class debate – 'For and Against Nationalisation'. Take a vote at the end.

C

An election poster, 1929.

 © Folens.

Glossary

Act (of Parliament) – law

Assassinate – murder, especially of a public or political figure.

Beveridge Report – 1942 report which led to the creation of the **Welfare State**

Bill – a written statement presented to **Parliament** to make a law

Budget – report on a country's finances

Cabinet – prime minister and chief ministers

Candidate – person who stands for **election** in a **constituency**

Capitalism – political belief in private ownership and personal wealth

Catholic (Roman) – Christian religion with the Pope as the head of the Church

Chancellor (of the Exchequer) – controls country's income and expenses, prepares the **budget**

Civil rights – fair treatment for everyone

Coalition – government of two or more parties

Commons (House of) – where elected **Members of Parliament** sit

Communism – system based on the common ownership of a country's wealth by the people (see **socialism**)

Communist – person or country supporting **communism**

Communist Party – ruling party of the former **USSR**

Congress – seat of government in the **USA**

Conservative Party – **political party** based on **right-wing** ideas

Constituency – place represented by an **MP**

Constitution – the rules or beliefs by which a country is governed

Democracy – rule by the people

Depression – period in which a country's income is low and unemployment is high; often refers to the period from 1929–1939

Discrimination – unequal and unfair treatment

Easter Rising – uprising by Irish Republics in 1916

Eire – Irish Free State, Southern Ireland

Election – choosing by voting

Executive – makes government policies

First past the post – voting system where the **candidate** with the most votes wins the seat

Franchise – the right to vote

General Strike – 1926, when people stopped work in protest for better conditions and pay

Home Rule – when a country governs itself but still belongs to another country

Home Secretary – minister for law and order

Immigrant – a person who settles in a country different from his or her place of birth

Independence – when a country governs itself but does not belong to another country

Irish Free State – Eire, Southern Ireland

Irish Republican Army (IRA) – **paramilitary** group

Judiciary – court of judges deciding the law

Labour Party – political party based on **left-wing** ideas (see **socialism**)

Law Lords – top judges

Left wing – political belief in individuals supporting one another (see **socialism**)

Legislature – decides laws and **policy**

Liberal Party – **political party** which believes in individual freedom, sometimes seen as half way between **Labour** and **Conservative**

Lords (House of) – where non-elected members of parliament sit

Loyalist – someone who wants to remain with the ruling country, loyal to the government

Majority – greater number

Martyr – someone who dies for a belief

Media – how information is passed to a large audience, e.g. film, television, newspapers

Glossary

Member of Parliament (MP) – person elected to the **House of Commons** to represent a **constituency**

Middle class – people in professions and business

Militant – someone who fights for a belief

Minority – small group

Multi-racial – many racial groups living side by side in one community

National Health Service (NHS) – system of free health care, part of the **Welfare State**

National Union of Women's Suffrage Societies (NUWSS) – a group formed in 1897 to campaign for votes for women

Nationalisation – putting industries under government control

Nationalist – someone who believes in their country's **independence**

One-party system – one **political party** in control

Paramilitary – group using violence for political reasons

Parliament – an assembly of **MPs**, the government

Partition – divide a country into parts

Peer – a member of the **House of Lords**

Policy – a government's course of action

Politburo – ruling group of the former **USSR**

Political party – group of people with the same political beliefs

Privatisation – putting industries under private control

Proportional Representation (PR) – voting system based on percentage vote for each **political party**

Protestant – Christian religion which broke from **Catholicism**

Reform – change made through law

Representative – a person who stands for something, or for a group

Republican – someone who believes in government without a king or queen

Right wing – political belief in individuals helping themselves

Sectarian – division between groups

Self-government – a country governing itself

Sinn Fein – Northern Ireland **Republican** party formed in 1905, linked to the **IRA**

Socialism – political belief in common ownership of a country's wealth and equal rights for everyone (see **communism)**

Suffragette – woman who fought for the vote in the early twentieth century (see **WSPU)**

Tory – another name for the **Conservatives**

Tory Socialist – a **Tory** who also believes that the state should provide for the people

Trade Union – association of workers who believe in protecting their rights

Trades Union Congress (TUC) – an association of **trade unions** formed in 1868

Treaty – agreement between two countries

Two-party system – two main **political parties** competing for power

Ulster – Northern Ireland

Unionist – someone who wants to remain united with the ruling country

USA – United States of America

USSR – the Union of Soviet Socialist Republics, the old name for Russia

Veto – the power to stop or say 'no'

Welfare State – a state or system which looks after its people

Women's Social and Political Union (WSPU) – a **militant** group formed in 1903 to campaign for women's rights

Working class – people in manual work

 © Folens.